MAD LIBS®

TRICK OR TREAT
MAD LIBS

by Tristan Roarke

MAD LIBS
An Imprint of Penguin Random House LLC, New York

Mad Libs format and text copyright © 2020 by Penguin Random House LLC.
All rights reserved.

Concept created by Roger Price & Leonard Stern

Cover illustration by Andrew Grey.

Published by Mad Libs,
an imprint of Penguin Random House LLC, New York.
Printed in the USA.

Visit us online at www.penguinrandomhouse.com.

ISBN 9780593096475
3 5 7 9 10 8 6 4

MAD LIBS®

INSTRUCTIONS

MAD LIBS® is a game for people who don't like games! It can be played by one, two, three, four, or forty.

• RIDICULOUSLY SIMPLE DIRECTIONS

In this tablet you will find stories containing blank spaces where words are left out. One player, the READER, selects one of these stories. The READER does not tell anyone what the story is about. Instead, he/she asks the other players, the WRITERS, to give him/her words. These words are used to fill in the blank spaces in the story.

• TO PLAY

The READER asks each WRITER in turn to call out a word—an adjective or a noun or whatever the space calls for—and uses them to fill in the blank spaces in the story. The result is a MAD LIBS® game.

When the READER then reads the completed MAD LIBS® game to the other players, they will discover that they have written a story that is fantastic, screamingly funny, shocking, silly, crazy, or just plain dumb—depending upon which words each WRITER called out.

• EXAMPLE (*Before* and *After*)

" _____ !" he said _____
       EXCLAMATION   ADVERB

as he jumped into his convertible _____ and
                                              NOUN

drove off with his _____ wife.
                            ADJECTIVE

" _____**OUCH**_____ !" he said _____**HAPPILY**_____
       EXCLAMATION   ADVERB

as he jumped into his convertible _____**CAT**_____ and
                                              NOUN

drove off with his _____**BRAVE**_____ wife.
                            ADJECTIVE

In case you have forgotten what adjectives, adverbs, nouns, and verbs are, here is a quick review:

An ADJECTIVE describes something or somebody. *Lumpy*, *soft*, *ugly*, *messy*, and *short* are adjectives.

An ADVERB tells how something is done. It modifies a verb and usually ends in "ly." *Modestly*, *stupidly*, *greedily*, and *carefully* are adverbs.

A NOUN is the name of a person, place, or thing. *Sidewalk*, *umbrella*, *bridle*, *bathtub*, and *nose* are nouns.

A VERB is an action word. *Run*, *pitch*, *jump*, and *swim* are verbs. Put the verbs in past tense if the directions say PAST TENSE. *Ran*, *pitched*, *jumped*, and *swam* are verbs in the past tense.

When we ask for A PLACE, we mean any sort of place: a country or city (*Spain*, *Cleveland*) or a room (*bathroom*, *kitchen*).

An EXCLAMATION or SILLY WORD is any sort of funny sound, gasp, grunt, or outcry, like *Wow!*, *Ouch!*, *Whomp!*, *Ick!*, and *Gadzooks!*

When we ask for specific words, like a NUMBER, a COLOR, an ANIMAL, or a PART OF THE BODY, we mean a word that is one of those things, like *seven*, *blue*, *horse*, or *head*.

When we ask for a PLURAL, it means more than one. For example, *cat* pluralized is *cats*.

MAD LIBS® is fun to play with friends, but you can also play it by yourself! To begin with, DO NOT look at the story on the page below. Fill in the blanks on this page with the words called for. Then, using the words you have selected, fill in the blank spaces in the story.

Now you've created your own hilarious MAD LIBS® game!

HAPPY HALLOWEEN!

NOUN _bag_

PLURAL NOUN _shirts_

OCCUPATION (PLURAL) _____

VERB _____

PLURAL NOUN _____

SILLY WORD _____

VERB ENDING IN "ING" _____

A PLACE _____

PLURAL NOUN _____

NOUN _____

SOMETHING ALIVE _____

VERB ENDING IN "ING" _____

TYPE OF FOOD _____

TYPE OF CONTAINER (PLURAL) _____

VERB _____

PART OF THE BODY _____

EXCLAMATION _____

MAD LIBS®

HAPPY HALLOWEEN!

Halloween is the best _____ of the year! I can't wait to dress
                          NOUN

up in scary _____ with my friends. This year, we're all
              PLURAL NOUN

being zombie _____ so we can _____ people in
              OCCUPATION (PLURAL)   VERB

the neighborhood. I'm wearing rotting green _____ on my
                                              PLURAL NOUN

face and will moan " _____ " everywhere I go. The best
                        SILLY WORD

part of Halloween is going trick-or- _____ around
                                      VERB ENDING IN "ING"

(the) _____ . Once night comes, we knock on people's
        A PLACE

_____ . When someone answers, we all shout
      PLURAL NOUN

" _____ or treat!" It's really fun when the _____
    NOUN   SOMETHING ALIVE

_____ the door gives us some sweet _____ .
VERB ENDING IN "ING"   TYPE OF FOOD

Then, we all slowly zombie-walk home with our pumpkin-shaped

_____ full of candy. I just wish zombies would
TYPE OF CONTAINER (PLURAL)

learn to not _____ all the candy at once so we don't end up
              VERB

with a/an _____ -ache. _____ !
          PART OF THE BODY   EXCLAMATION

MAD LIBS® is fun to play with friends, but you can also play it by yourself! To begin with, DO NOT look at the story on the page below. Fill in the blanks on this page with the words called for. Then, using the words you have selected, fill in the blank spaces in the story.

Now you've created your own hilarious MAD LIBS® game!

BAG OR BUCKET?

VERB ENDING IN "ING" _____

TYPE OF FOOD _____

OCCUPATION (PLURAL) _____

ADJECTIVE _____

COLOR _____

ADJECTIVE _____

A PLACE _____

NOUN _____

NOUN _____

ADVERB _____

NUMBER _____

VERB _____

NOUN _____

VERB _____

TYPE OF FOOD _____

A PLACE (PLURAL) _____

NOUN _____

ADJECTIVE _____

MAD LIBS®

BAG OR BUCKET?

Halloween is all about _____ candy! Here are some tips
VERB ENDING IN "ING"

to help you get as much _____ as you can from all the
TYPE OF FOOD

_____ in your neighborhood. The most important thing
OCCUPATION (PLURAL)

to do is pick out a/an _____ candy bucket. Usually they're
ADJECTIVE

shaped like a/an _____ pumpkin. But if you really want to be
COLOR

a/an _____ trick-or-treater, go to your _____ and get
ADJECTIVE   A PLACE

a pillow- _____ from your bed. Of course, you'll need to take
NOUN

out the comfy _____ to make room for all your candy, but it's
NOUN

_____ worth it. A pillowcase can hold _____
ADVERB   NUMBER

pounds more candy than you could ever _____ in a/an
VERB

_____! Then _____ the pavement and start demanding
NOUN   VERB

_____! Go to as many _____ as you can and shout
TYPE OF FOOD   A PLACE (PLURAL)

"trick or _____!" before the night is _____!
NOUN   ADJECTIVE

MAD LIBS® is fun to play with friends, but you can also play it by yourself! To begin with, DO NOT look at the story on the page below. Fill in the blanks on this page with the words called for. Then, using the words you have selected, fill in the blank spaces in the story.

Now you've created your own hilarious MAD LIBS® game!

NO COSTUME?
NO PROBLEM!

NOUN _____

ADJECTIVE _____

ADJECTIVE _____

NOUN _____

PART OF THE BODY _____

PART OF THE BODY _____

VERB _____

OCCUPATION _____

PLURAL NOUN _____

NOUN _____

ADJECTIVE _____

NOUN _____

NOUN _____

ANIMAL _____

ARTICLE OF CLOTHING _____

TYPE OF FOOD _____

TYPE OF LIQUID _____

So, you forgot to buy a/an _____ for Halloween this year?
                           NOUN

Here are some _____ costume ideas to make your night of
               ADJECTIVE

trick-or-treating _____!
                   ADJECTIVE

- If you want to be a ghost, just get a/an _____ from your
                                            NOUN

  bedroom and put it over your _____. Don't forget to
                                PART OF THE BODY

  cut _____-holes or you won't be able to _____ .
      PART OF THE BODY   VERB

- It's easy to be an ancient _____ . Just get some stretchy
                              OCCUPATION

  _____ and wrap your entire _____ until it's
  PLURAL NOUN   NOUN

  completely covered.

- If you want to trick-or-treat as a/an _____ vampire, get a
                                         ADJECTIVE

  black _____ from your linen closet and wear it as a spooky
         NOUN

  _____ .
  NOUN

- Want to be a headless _____-man? Just button your
                         ANIMAL

  _____ over your head and add some _____
  ARTICLE OF CLOTHING   TYPE OF FOOD

  on the collar to look like _____ .
                             TYPE OF LIQUID

From TRICK OR TREAT MAD LIBS® • Copyright © 2020 by Penguin Random House LLC.

MAD LIBS® is fun to play with friends, but you can also play it by yourself! To begin with, DO NOT look at the story on the page below. Fill in the blanks on this page with the words called for. Then, using the words you have selected, fill in the blank spaces in the story.

Now you've created your own hilarious MAD LIBS® game!

HALLOWEEN WINNERS AND LOSERS

CELEBRITY _____

VERB ENDING IN "ING" _____

ADJECTIVE _____

A PLACE _____

NOUN _____

ANIMAL _____

ADJECTIVE _____

VERB _____

OCCUPATION _____

TYPE OF FOOD _____

VERB (PAST TENSE) _____

PLURAL NOUN _____

ADJECTIVE _____

ADJECTIVE _____

TYPE OF FOOD (PLURAL) _____

PLURAL NOUN _____

TYPE OF FOOD (PLURAL) _____

ADJECTIVE _____

MAD LIBS
HALLOWEEN
WINNERS AND LOSERS

Hello, my name is _____ . There's nothing I love more than
_____ CELEBRITY on a costume and going trick-or-treating!
VERB ENDING IN "ING"

This year, I got some pretty _____ candy! The owners of (the)
ADJECTIVE

_____ next door gave me a chocolate-covered _____
A PLACE NOUN

shaped like a/an _____ . It looked so _____ , I
ANIMAL ADJECTIVE

couldn't wait to get home and _____ it! My other next-door
VERB

_____ gave me the yummiest candy bar ever. It was covered
OCCUPATION

with crunchy _____ that _____ every time
TYPE OF FOOD VERB (PAST TENSE)

I took a bite. Of course, not all the _____ I got were
PLURAL NOUN

_____ . There always seems to be that one house that gives
ADJECTIVE

out _____ _____ instead of candy. One
ADJECTIVE TYPE OF FOOD (PLURAL)

year, they gave everyone red _____ from a tree in their yard,
PLURAL NOUN

and this year they gave out slices of ripe _____
TYPE OF FOOD (PLURAL)

because they said they wanted us to be " _____ ."
ADJECTIVE

MAD LIBS® is fun to play with friends, but you can also play it by yourself! To begin with, DO NOT look at the story on the page below. Fill in the blanks on this page with the words called for. Then, using the words you have selected, fill in the blank spaces in the story.

Now you've created your own hilarious MAD LIBS® game!

TRICK OR TREAT TACTICS

ADJECTIVE _____

TYPE OF FOOD (PLURAL) _____

VERB (PAST TENSE) _____

NOUN _____

ADJECTIVE _____

ADJECTIVE _____

VERB _____

NUMBER _____

VERB ENDING IN "ING" _____

EXCLAMATION _____

PLURAL NOUN _____

PLURAL NOUN _____

FIRST NAME _____

TYPE OF FOOD _____

TYPE OF BUILDING _____

ADJECTIVE _____

SAME TYPE OF BUILDING _____

MAD LIBS®

TRICK OR TREAT TACTICS

Here are some _____ tips to get lots of _____
         <u>ADJECTIVE</u>   <u>TYPE OF FOOD (PLURAL)</u>

when you go trick-or-treating on Halloween:

- People love costumes that they've never _____ before.
                                            <u>VERB (PAST TENSE)</u>

   Choose to wear a/an _____ that's original and _____ .
                        <u>NOUN</u>   <u>ADJECTIVE</u>

- Try on your _____ costume ahead of time to be sure you
                 <u>ADJECTIVE</u>

   can _____ around easily. It won't be easy to walk if your
        <u>VERB</u>

   costume weighs _____ pounds or if you can't see where you're
                   <u>NUMBER</u>

   _____ .
   <u>VERB ENDING IN "ING"</u>

- Be polite and say "_____!" after someone puts
                        <u>EXCLAMATION</u>

   _____ in your bag.
   <u>PLURAL NOUN</u>

- Go to a house with lots of Halloween _____ taped up
                                          <u>PLURAL NOUN</u>

   all over it. Lots of _____ -o'-lanterns are also a sure
                         <u>FIRST NAME</u>

   sign that there's _____ inside that house.
                      <u>TYPE OF FOOD</u>

- Never go to a/an _____ if the lights are
                    <u>TYPE OF BUILDING</u>

   _____ . This either means no one's home or that it's a
   <u>ADJECTIVE</u>

   haunted _____ .
            <u>SAME TYPE OF BUILDING</u>

MAD LIBS® is fun to play with friends, but you can also play it by yourself! To begin with, DO NOT look at the story on the page below. Fill in the blanks on this page with the words called for. Then, using the words you have selected, fill in the blank spaces in the story.

Now you've created your own hilarious MAD LIBS® game!

HALLOWEEN TIME MACHINE

ADJECTIVE _____

SILLY WORD _____

OCCUPATION _____

NOUN _____

ADJECTIVE _____

NUMBER _____

ADJECTIVE _____

VERB _____

A PLACE _____

PLURAL NOUN _____

TYPE OF FOOD _____

ADJECTIVE _____

ADJECTIVE _____

VERB _____

NOUN _____

TYPE OF FOOD (PLURAL) _____

EXCLAMATION _____

ADJECTIVE _____

MAD LIBS®
HALLOWEEN
TIME MACHINE

Here's a/an _____ interview with the world's oldest trick-or-
ADJECTIVE

treater:

Interviewer: Hello, today I'm talking with Olga von _____ ,
SILLY WORD

the world's oldest _____ . Tell me, Olga, what was Halloween
OCCUPATION

like when you were a young _____ ?
NOUN

Olga: Oh, very, very _____ ! _____ years ago, when I
ADJECTIVE   NUMBER

was _____ , instead of walking from house to house, you had
ADJECTIVE

to _____ from farm to _____ . I had to walk over
VERB   A PLACE

twenty _____ in one night just to get two pieces of
PLURAL NOUN

_____ .
TYPE OF FOOD

Interviewer: Wow. That sounds absolutely _____ !
ADJECTIVE

Olga: And that's not even the _____ part. Instead of carrying
ADJECTIVE

a plastic pumpkin, you had to _____ a heavy wooden
VERB

_____ , and people only handed out stale _____ .
NOUN   TYPE OF FOOD (PLURAL)

Interviewer: _____ . It sounds like kids today don't know
EXCLAMATION

how _____ they are!
ADJECTIVE

MAD LIBS® is fun to play with friends, but you can also play it by yourself! To begin with, DO NOT look at the story on the page below. Fill in the blanks on this page with the words called for. Then, using the words you have selected, fill in the blank spaces in the story.

Now you've created your own hilarious MAD LIBS® game!

ALIEN REPORT!

VERB ENDING IN "ING" _____

EXCLAMATION _____

SILLY WORD _____

ADJECTIVE _____

NOUN _____

SOMETHING ALIVE (PLURAL) _____

ARTICLE OF CLOTHING (PLURAL) _____

PART OF THE BODY (PLURAL) _____

ADJECTIVE _____

VERB _____

ADJECTIVE _____

ANIMAL (PLURAL) _____

NOUN _____

PLURAL NOUN _____

PART OF THE BODY _____

VEHICLE _____

VERB _____

VERB ENDING IN "ING" _____

MAD LIBS®

ALIEN REPORT!

An alien who is _____ Halloween reports back to her
          VERB ENDING IN "ING"

home planet:

Gleeglorg: _____ , Grand Commander _____ .
        EXCLAMATION   SILLY WORD

I'm reporting my findings on the _____ Earth holiday called
                ADJECTIVE

Halloween. On this _____ , small _____
            NOUN   SOMETHING ALIVE (PLURAL)

like to take the _____ from a different creature
       ARTICLE OF CLOTHING (PLURAL)

and put them on their own _____ .
            PART OF THE BODY (PLURAL)

Fleeflorg: Hmmm. That's very _____ behavior.
                ADJECTIVE

Gleeglorg: Then they _____ in the dark to houses with
              VERB

many _____ skeletons and were- _____ placed in
    ADJECTIVE   ANIMAL (PLURAL)

the front yard.

Fleeflorg: Thank you for your _____ , Gleeglorg. This report
                NOUN

is sending _____ down my _____ . Return to
       PLURAL NOUN   PART OF THE BODY

the safety of your space _____ at once.
            VEHICLE

Gleeglorg: As you _____ , Grand Commander.
              VERB

_____ transmission.
VERB ENDING IN "ING"

MAD LIBS® is fun to play with friends, but you can also play it by yourself! To begin with, DO NOT look at the story on the page below. Fill in the blanks on this page with the words called for. Then, using the words you have selected, fill in the blank spaces in the story.

Now you've created your own hilarious MAD LIBS® game!

DEVIOUS DECORATING

ADJECTIVE _____

VERB ENDING IN "ING" _____

ADJECTIVE _____

A PLACE _____

ADJECTIVE _____

PLURAL NOUN _____

PART OF THE BODY (PLURAL) _____

SOMETHING ALIVE (PLURAL) _____

VERB _____

VERB _____

PLURAL NOUN _____

SOMETHING ALIVE (PLURAL) _____

ADJECTIVE _____

NOUN _____

EXCLAMATION _____

VERB _____

TYPE OF FOOD (PLURAL) _____

PLURAL NOUN _____

MAD LIBS

DEVIOUS DECORATING

On Halloween, you want your house to look as _____ as
ADJECTIVE

possible to scare the trick-or-treaters who come _____
VERB ENDING IN "ING"

for candy. One _____ idea is to turn your front yard into a
ADJECTIVE

haunted _____ . You can do this by making _____
A PLACE   ADJECTIVE

tombstones out of cardboard _____ and placing them
PLURAL NOUN

around the yard. Then add plastic _____ sticking
PART OF THE BODY (PLURAL)

out of the dirt in front of the tombstones so it looks like spooky

_____ are trying to _____ their way to the
SOMETHING ALIVE (PLURAL)   VERB

surface and _____ the trick-or-treaters. Next, hang as many
VERB

spider- _____ as you can from the _____
PLURAL NOUN   SOMETHING ALIVE (PLURAL)

and bushes, and play _____ music. When the trick-or-treaters
ADJECTIVE

come, jump out from behind a/an _____ and shout
NOUN

" _____ !" This should make the trick-or-treaters
EXCLAMATION

_____ , but don't worry: They'll feel better once you put
VERB

_____ in their _____ .
TYPE OF FOOD (PLURAL)   PLURAL NOUN

MAD LIBS® is fun to play with friends, but you can also play it by yourself! To begin with, DO NOT look at the story on the page below. Fill in the blanks on this page with the words called for. Then, using the words you have selected, fill in the blank spaces in the story.

Now you've created your own hilarious MAD LIBS® game!

TREAT *AND* TRICK!

OCCUPATION _____

ADJECTIVE _____

TYPE OF BUILDING _____

NOUN _____

ARTICLE OF CLOTHING _____

TYPE OF FOOD (PLURAL) _____

ADVERB _____

VERB (PAST TENSE) _____

ADJECTIVE _____

ANIMAL _____

PART OF THE BODY (PLURAL) _____

NOUN _____

VERB _____

PART OF THE BODY _____

PART OF THE BODY _____

EXCLAMATION _____

VERB ENDING IN "ING" _____

VERB _____

MAD◉LIBS®

TREAT *AND* TRICK!

Last Halloween, my best _____ and I went trick-or-treating
_{OCCUPATION}

at a/an _____ _____. All the kids in the
_{ADJECTIVE} _{TYPE OF BUILDING}

neighborhood thought the woman who lived there was a wicked

_____. But we hoped she was just wearing a really good
_{NOUN}

Halloween _____. The witch gave us some strange
_{ARTICLE OF CLOTHING}

_____ to eat. My best friend _____
_{TYPE OF FOOD (PLURAL)} _{ADVERB}

_____ the treats and then something _____
_{VERB (PAST TENSE)} _{ADJECTIVE}

happened—he turned into a/an _____, right in front of my
_{ANIMAL}

_____! At first, I thought this was just some type of
_{PART OF THE BODY (PLURAL)}

magic _____, but then he started to _____ like a
_{NOUN} _{VERB}

frog, too. He even grabbed my _____ and tried to bite my
_{PART OF THE BODY}

_____. "_____!" I shouted, before
_{PART OF THE BODY} _{EXCLAMATION}

_____ down the street. That's the last time I ever
_{VERB ENDING IN "ING"}

_____ on a witch's door.
_{VERB}

MAD LIBS® is fun to play with friends, but you can also play it by yourself! To begin with, DO NOT look at the story on the page below. Fill in the blanks on this page with the words called for. Then, using the words you have selected, fill in the blank spaces in the story.

Now you've created your own hilarious MAD LIBS® game!

CREEPY TREATS

ADJECTIVE _____

TYPE OF BUILDING _____

VERB _____

COLOR _____

PART OF THE BODY (PLURAL) _____

ADJECTIVE _____

ANIMAL (PLURAL) _____

PART OF THE BODY (PLURAL) _____

ADJECTIVE _____

VERB _____

VERB _____

PART OF THE BODY (PLURAL) _____

COLOR _____

TYPE OF FOOD (PLURAL) _____

NOUN _____

NOUN _____

MAD LIBS®

CREEPY TREATS

One of the _____ things about Halloween is making
ADJECTIVE

_____-made treats. Here are some ideas that'll make
TYPE OF BUILDING

kids _____ with joy!
VERB

- Bake _____ cookies with lots of _____
  COLOR   PART OF THE BODY (PLURAL)

  so they look like _____ black widow _____.
  ADJECTIVE   ANIMAL (PLURAL)

- Attach a pair of paper _____ to the sides of a
  PART OF THE BODY (PLURAL)

  cupcake to make it look like a/an _____ bat, ready to
  ADJECTIVE

  _____ through the sky!
  VERB

- You can _____ broken candy canes into a vampire cookie
  VERB

  so they look like sharp _____.
  PART OF THE BODY (PLURAL)

- Take a/an _____ apple and dip it in melted white
  COLOR

  _____. Then push a/an _____ into the
  TYPE OF FOOD (PLURAL)   NOUN

  center and serve it upside down as a ghostly _____!
  NOUN

MAD LIBS® is fun to play with friends, but you can also play it by yourself! To begin with, DO NOT look at the story on the page below. Fill in the blanks on this page with the words called for. Then, using the words you have selected, fill in the blank spaces in the story.

Now you've created your own hilarious MAD LIBS® game!

FRANKENSTEIN'S DIARY

VERB ENDING IN "ING" _____

ADJECTIVE _____

NOUN _____

PLURAL NOUN _____

SOMETHING ALIVE (PLURAL) _____

VERB ENDING IN "ING" _____

NOUN _____

TYPE OF EVENT _____

VERB _____

ADJECTIVE _____

TYPE OF FOOD (PLURAL) _____

SOMETHING ALIVE _____

ARTICLE OF CLOTHING _____

NOUN _____

PART OF THE BODY _____

SILLY WORD _____

PLURAL NOUN _____

NOUN _____

MAD LIBS®

FRANKENSTEIN'S DIARY

Dear Diary. Today me have fun and go trick-or-_____

VERB ENDING IN "ING"

for first time. Good news is, face already look _____ , so me

ADJECTIVE

not have to wear Halloween _____ . Me see kids dressed as

NOUN

_____ and _____ . No one afraid of me

PLURAL NOUN   SOMETHING ALIVE (PLURAL)

because they think me _____ fake _____ .

VERB ENDING IN "ING"   NOUN

Next, me go with kids to Halloween _____ . There,

TYPE OF EVENT

everyone _____ to _____ music and play Halloween

VERB   ADJECTIVE

games, like bobbing for _____ . Me have lots of

TYPE OF FOOD (PLURAL)

fun dancing with _____ . Then, me win best

SOMETHING ALIVE

_____ contest. When villagers try to take off me

ARTICLE OF CLOTHING

_____ , they realize it really me _____ . They

NOUN   PART OF THE BODY

scream "_____!" and chase me away with pitchforks and

SILLY WORD

_____ . Me love Halloween and next year me want to go

PLURAL NOUN

trick-or-treating dressed as a friendly _____ .

NOUN

MAD LIBS® is fun to play with friends, but you can also play it by yourself! To begin with, DO NOT look at the story on the page below. Fill in the blanks on this page with the words called for. Then, using the words you have selected, fill in the blank spaces in the story.

Now you've created your own hilarious MAD LIBS® game!

TOIL AND TROUBLE

NOUN _____

PART OF THE BODY (PLURAL) _____

PART OF THE BODY _____

ANIMAL _____

NUMBER _____

NOUN _____

ADJECTIVE _____

TYPE OF LIQUID _____

TYPE OF FOOD (PLURAL) _____

VERB _____

NOUN _____

NUMBER _____

TYPE OF CONTAINER _____

VERB ENDING IN "ING" _____

NOUN _____

TOIL AND TROUBLE

Hello, fellow witches! Here's a recipe to whip up a wicked _____
NOUN

that'll put a smile on those pesky kids' _____ when
PART OF THE BODY (PLURAL)

they come to your door on Halloween.

1. Take one _____ of a/an _____ and mix it with
    PART OF THE BODY   ANIMAL

    _____ pinches of _____ .
    NUMBER   NOUN

2. Pour in _____ _____ and blend until it smells
    ADJECTIVE   TYPE OF LIQUID

    like fried _____ .
    TYPE OF FOOD (PLURAL)

3. _____ all the ingredients in an iron _____ .
    VERB   NOUN

    Once cooked, put _____ drops of the potion in a/an
    NUMBER

    _____ and give it to any child who comes to your
    TYPE OF CONTAINER

    door _____ for a yummy _____ .
    VERB ENDING IN "ING"   NOUN

MAD LIBS® is fun to play with friends, but you can also play it by yourself! To begin with, DO NOT look at the story on the page below. Fill in the blanks on this page with the words called for. Then, using the words you have selected, fill in the blank spaces in the story.

Now you've created your own hilarious MAD LIBS® game!

HISTORY OF TRICK-OR-TREATING

COUNTRY _____

NUMBER _____

VERB (PAST TENSE) _____

PLURAL NOUN _____

SILLY WORD _____

SAME SILLY WORD _____

PART OF THE BODY (PLURAL) _____

PLURAL NOUN _____

ADJECTIVE _____

TYPE OF FOOD (PLURAL) _____

TYPE OF LIQUID (PLURAL) _____

SOMETHING ALIVE (PLURAL) _____

VERB _____

ADJECTIVE _____

VERB _____

TYPE OF FOOD (PLURAL) _____

TYPE OF EVENT _____

MAD LIBS
HISTORY OF
TRICK-OR-TREATING

Trick-or-treating is a custom that started in _____ nearly
                                              COUNTRY

_____ years ago. The people who _____ during
     NUMBER   VERB (PAST TENSE)

that time believed that creepy _____ returned to earth
                                    PLURAL NOUN

once a year to cause mischief. They called this night _____.
                                                          SILLY WORD

As part of this event, the people created the festival of

_____. During the festival, villagers would dress themselves
SAME SILLY WORD

in animal _____ to drive away evil _____.
           PART OF THE BODY (PLURAL)   PLURAL NOUN

_____ banquet tables were filled with delicious
      ADJECTIVE

_____ and warm _____, and
TYPE OF FOOD (PLURAL)   TYPE OF LIQUID (PLURAL)

were meant to appease any hungry _____ that would
                                  SOMETHING ALIVE (PLURAL)

_____ the earth on that _____ night. Centuries later,
    VERB   ADJECTIVE

kids began to _____ from house to house and ask for
                    VERB

_____ to celebrate the same ritual. Today, this
TYPE OF FOOD (PLURAL)

custom is celebrated in places around the world as the _____
                                                         TYPE OF EVENT

of Halloween.

MAD LIBS® is fun to play with friends, but you can also play it by yourself! To begin with, DO NOT look at the story on the page below. Fill in the blanks on this page with the words called for. Then, using the words you have selected, fill in the blank spaces in the story.

Now you've created your own hilarious MAD LIBS® game!

CANDY COMMERCIAL

ADJECTIVE _____

SOMETHING ALIVE (PLURAL) _____

TYPE OF FOOD (PLURAL) _____

NOUN _____

SILLY WORD _____

VERB _____

NOUN _____

PART OF THE BODY (PLURAL) _____

TYPE OF FOOD (PLURAL) _____

NUMBER _____

TYPE OF FOOD (PLURAL) _____

NOUN _____

PART OF THE BODY _____

VERB _____

TYPE OF FOOD (PLURAL) _____

PLURAL NOUN _____

VERB (PAST TENSE) _____

MAD LIBS

CANDY COMMERCIAL

Are you tired of handing out the same _____ candy every year
_____ADJECTIVE_____

on Halloween? Do all the _____ skip your house
_____SOMETHING ALIVE (PLURAL)_____

when they trick-or-treat because the _____ you
_____TYPE OF FOOD (PLURAL)_____

hand out are as tasty as an old _____? Well, come on down
_____NOUN_____

to Ted's _____ Candy Shop! Our candy experts lovingly
_____SILLY WORD_____

_____ each delicious _____ with their own
____VERB_____NOUN_____

_____. All our _____ are covered
PART OF THE BODY (PLURAL)_____TYPE OF FOOD (PLURAL)_____

in _____ percent yummy yumminess! And Ted's lollipops are
____NUMBER_____

filled with chewy _____that'll let you blow the
_____TYPE OF FOOD (PLURAL)_____

biggest _____ you've ever seen! Once the trick-or-treaters see
_____NOUN_____

you pull out one of our famous _____-breakers,
_____PART OF THE BODY_____

they'll _____ with delight! One bite of any of our
_____VERB_____

_____ and the kids in your neighborhood will say
TYPE OF FOOD (PLURAL)_____

your family hands out the best _____ they've ever
_____PLURAL NOUN_____

_____.
VERB (PAST TENSE)

MAD LIBS® is fun to play with friends, but you can also play it by yourself! To begin with, DO NOT look at the story on the page below. Fill in the blanks on this page with the words called for. Then, using the words you have selected, fill in the blank spaces in the story.

Now you've created your own hilarious MAD LIBS® game!

EXPRESS YOURSELF!

VERB _____

VERB _____

PLURAL NOUN _____

PART OF THE BODY (PLURAL) _____

ADJECTIVE _____

ARTICLE OF CLOTHING _____

SILLY WORD _____

OCCUPATION _____

NOUN _____

VERB _____

ADJECTIVE _____

ARTICLE OF CLOTHING _____

PART OF THE BODY _____

NOUN _____

VERB _____

NOUN _____

VERB _____

PLURAL NOUN _____

Halloween is a great chance to dress up as the thing you _____
                                                          VERB

most! It's a night when ghosts _____ the neighborhoods, and
                                   VERB

undead _____ roam the streets in search of human
          PLURAL NOUN

_____ to eat. Of course, not all costumes need to
PART OF THE BODY (PLURAL)

be _____. If you want to be a cowboy, just put a/an
        ADJECTIVE

_____ on your head and shout "Yee-_____!"
ARTICLE OF CLOTHING   SILLY WORD

If you've always wanted to be a super-_____, put on a/an
                                          OCCUPATION

_____ and pretend you can _____ through the sky.
   NOUN   VERB

A princess is another _____ costume. If that's more your
                          ADJECTIVE

speed, just wear a long, flowing _____ and put a
                                    ARTICLE OF CLOTHING

crown on your _____. You can even dress as something
                 PART OF THE BODY

silly, like a/an _____, to make people _____.
                    NOUN   VERB

Whatever _____ you choose to wear, just remember that the
             NOUN

most important thing is to _____ yourself and have a fun
                              VERB

night with your best _____!
                         PLURAL NOUN

MAD LIBS® is fun to play with friends, but you can also play it by yourself! To begin with, DO NOT look at the story on the page below. Fill in the blanks on this page with the words called for. Then, using the words you have selected, fill in the blank spaces in the story.

Now you've created your own hilarious MAD LIBS® game!

HOWLING BEAUTY

ADJECTIVE _____

VERB ENDING IN "ING" _____

SOMETHING ALIVE _____

PART OF THE BODY _____

NUMBER _____

ADJECTIVE _____

EXCLAMATION _____

PART OF THE BODY (PLURAL) _____

VERB _____

VERB _____

TYPE OF LIQUID _____

ADJECTIVE _____

VERB _____

ADJECTIVE _____

VERB _____

MAD LIBS®

HOWLING BEAUTY

Even a werewolf wants to look _____ when they go trick-
                                    ADJECTIVE
or-_____ on Halloween night. Here are some helpful
      VERB ENDING IN "ING"
tips for the _____ in everyone!
               SOMETHING ALIVE

- Make sure to comb your _____ at least _____
                              PART OF THE BODY   NUMBER
  times so your fur is nice and _____ .
                                      ADJECTIVE

- Nothing says "_____!" like bright, shiny
                              EXCLAMATION
  _____! So before you go out, use a toothbrush
  PART OF THE BODY (PLURAL)
  to _____ your fangs until they're gleaming white.
         VERB

- If you really want to _____ at the moon, make sure
                               VERB
  to drink plenty of warm _____ so your voice is
                                    TYPE OF LIQUID
  _____ .
     ADJECTIVE

- And what werewolf doesn't love to _____ to some music?
                                           VERB
  Make sure you get some _____ shoes so you can
                                  ADJECTIVE
  _____ the night away!
       VERB

MAD LIBS® is fun to play with friends, but you can also play it by yourself! To begin with, DO NOT look at the story on the page below. Fill in the blanks on this page with the words called for. Then, using the words you have selected, fill in the blank spaces in the story.

Now you've created your own hilarious MAD LIBS® game!

PUMPKIN IT UP

VERB ENDING IN "ING" _____

PLURAL NOUN _____

NOUN _____

PART OF THE BODY (PLURAL) _____

PART OF THE BODY _____

NOUN _____

ADJECTIVE _____

TYPE OF FOOD _____

ADJECTIVE _____

NOUN _____

PLURAL NOUN _____

PLURAL NOUN _____

ADJECTIVE _____

NOUN _____

NOUN _____

VERB _____

NOUN _____

PUMPKIN IT UP

Check out these steps for _____ a pumpkin that will
 VERB ENDING IN "ING"

scare the _____ that come to your _____ on
 PLURAL NOUN NOUN

Halloween:

1. Once you've selected your pumpkin, use a marker to draw

    _____ and a/an _____ on the
    PART OF THE BODY (PLURAL) PART OF THE BODY

    pumpkin's _____ . Some people like to carve a/an
     NOUN

    _____ face, while others prefer making the _____
    ADJECTIVE TYPE OF FOOD

    look silly.

2. Next, ask an adult to get a/an _____ _____ ,
     ADJECTIVE NOUN

    so they can carefully cut the pumpkin along the marker lines.

    Remove the pumpkin's inner _____ and clean out all
     PLURAL NOUN

    the sticky _____ growing inside.
     PLURAL NOUN

3. Light up your jack-o'-lantern with a/an _____ glow
     ADJECTIVE

    by putting a battery-operated _____ inside the pumpkin,
     NOUN

    then place the pumpkin on your _____ . Finally, sit
     NOUN

    back and _____ your scary _____ !
     VERB NOUN

MAD LIBS® is fun to play with friends, but you can also play it by yourself! To begin with, DO NOT look at the story on the page below. Fill in the blanks on this page with the words called for. Then, using the words you have selected, fill in the blank spaces in the story.

Now you've created your own hilarious MAD LIBS® game!

TRICK OR TREAT
SAFETY TIPS

NOUN _____

ADJECTIVE _____

ADVERB _____

VERB ENDING IN "S" _____

PLURAL NOUN _____

VERB ENDING IN "ING" _____

NOUN _____

PLURAL NOUN _____

VEHICLE (PLURAL) _____

OCCUPATION _____

VERB _____

PLURAL NOUN _____

NOUN _____

VERB _____

TYPE OF BUILDING (PLURAL) _____

TYPE OF FOOD _____

MAD☺LIBS®
TRICK OR TREAT
SAFETY TIPS

Here is a step-by-_____ guide to help you stay safe and
NOUN

_____ on Halloween night!
ADJECTIVE

- Make sure your Halloween costume fits and is zipped up

  _____ . No one wants to be the mummy who
  ADVERB

  _____ over their own _____ .
  VERB ENDING IN "S"   PLURAL NOUN

- Since you'll be _____ in the dark, carry a bright
  VERB ENDING IN "ING"

  _____ with you. That way you can see any _____
  NOUN   PLURAL NOUN

  in your path, and you can be seen by passing _____ .
  VEHICLE (PLURAL)

- Take a parent or _____ with you, and always
  OCCUPATION

  _____ in a group. Halloween is more fun with a group of
  VERB

  _____ anyway!
  PLURAL NOUN

- Use a/an _____ to plan your route and _____ the
  NOUN   VERB

  _____ in your neighborhood early. That way,
  TYPE OF BUILDING (PLURAL)

  you'll have enough time to count your _____ before
  TYPE OF FOOD

  bedtime.

MAD LIBS® is fun to play with friends, but you can also play it by yourself! To begin with, DO NOT look at the story on the page below. Fill in the blanks on this page with the words called for. Then, using the words you have selected, fill in the blank spaces in the story.

Now you've created your own hilarious MAD LIBS® game!

HALLOVEEN BITES!

SILLY WORD _____

SOMETHING ALIVE _____

VERB _____

VERB _____

PLURAL NOUN _____

A PLACE (PLURAL) _____

PLURAL NOUN _____

TYPE OF FOOD (PLURAL) _____

ADJECTIVE _____

PART OF THE BODY _____

ADJECTIVE _____

ANIMAL _____

PART OF THE BODY (PLURAL) _____

NOUN _____

PART OF THE BODY (PLURAL) _____

NOUN _____

VERB (PAST TENSE) _____

CELEBRITY _____

MAD LIBS®

HALLOVEEN BITES!

Good evening. I am the vampire Count _____. You vould
                                      SILLY WORD
think that because I'm a/an _____ of the night,
                              SOMETHING ALIVE
Halloveen vould be my favorite time of year. But the truth is, vampires

_____ Halloveen! Usually, vhen people see me, they
          VERB
_____ and run avay! But on Halloveen, children dressed as
    VERB
_____ vander (the) _____, holding out
        PLURAL NOUN   A PLACE (PLURAL)
their little hands, demanding _____. If I do not give
                                  PLURAL NOUN
them _____, they pull a trick on me, like pouring
       TYPE OF FOOD (PLURAL)
something _____ on my _____. One time
              ADJECTIVE   PART OF THE BODY
I became so _____, I turned into a/an _____
                ADJECTIVE   ANIMAL
and tried to bite their _____. "I vant to
                            PART OF THE BODY (PLURAL)
suck your _____," I hissed as I showed them
                  NOUN
my _____. But the dreadful little children thought
     PART OF THE BODY (PLURAL)
I vas just vearing a/an _____, and they _____
                            NOUN   VERB (PAST TENSE)
at me! On nights like these, I vish I vas _____ instead
                                             CELEBRITY
of a vampire.

MAD LIBS® is fun to play with friends, but you can also play it by yourself! To begin with, DO NOT look at the story on the page below. Fill in the blanks on this page with the words called for. Then, using the words you have selected, fill in the blank spaces in the story.

Now you've created your own hilarious MAD LIBS® game!

HALLOWEEN MOVIE MADNESS

VERB _____

NOUN _____

NOUN _____

ADJECTIVE _____

VERB _____

PLURAL NOUN _____

TYPE OF FOOD _____

SOMETHING ALIVE _____

VERB ENDING IN "ING" _____

VERB _____

PLURAL NOUN _____

VERB _____

A PLACE (PLURAL) _____

CELEBRITY _____

LAST NAME _____

CELEBRITY _____

PERSON IN ROOM _____

MAD LIBS®
HALLOWEEN MOVIE MADNESS

Do you dare to _____ the most frightening movie of the year:
                        VERB

Night of the Living _____ ? It's the Halloween horror
                              NOUN

_____ you've been waiting for! Follow the _____
        NOUN   ADJECTIVE

story of three best friends as they _____ around their
                                            VERB

neighborhood on Halloween. What starts out as a fun evening turns

into a nightmare of epic _____ when the friends unwrap
                              PLURAL NOUN

a Halloween _____ and discover an evil _____
                TYPE OF FOOD   SOMETHING ALIVE

_____ inside! You'll never _____ with the
VERB ENDING IN "ING"   VERB

lights off again after seeing the trick-or-treaters in a haunted house

filled with possessed _____! These three unfortunate friends
                          PLURAL NOUN

must _____ for their lives if they ever hope to see their
            VERB

_____ again! Starring _____ as
    A PLACE (PLURAL)   CELEBRITY

Karen _____ and _____ in the role of a lifetime
            LAST NAME   CELEBRITY

as _____ .
    PERSON IN ROOM

From TRICK OR TREAT MAD LIBS® • Copyright © 2020 by Penguin Random House LLC.

MAD LIBS® is fun to play with friends, but you can also play it by yourself! To begin with, DO NOT look at the story on the page below. Fill in the blanks on this page with the words called for. Then, using the words you have selected, fill in the blank spaces in the story.

Now you've created your own hilarious MAD LIBS® game!

TREATS AND NO TRICKS

NOUN _____

ADJECTIVE _____

NOUN _____

NOUN _____

ADJECTIVE _____

VERB ENDING IN "ING" _____

VERB _____

NOUN _____

VERB ENDING IN "S" _____

TYPE OF LIQUID _____

VERB _____

TYPE OF FOOD _____

PART OF THE BODY _____

VERB _____

NOUN _____

MAD LIBS

TREATS AND NO TRICKS

Sometimes it's hard to tell if a trick-or-treater is just wearing a/an

_____ or if they are the real thing! Here's a/an _____
         NOUN   ADJECTIVE

quiz to see if you can tell the difference between what's real and what's

a/an _____ !
          NOUN

1. The best way to tell if a wizard is real, and not just a/an

   _____ in a costume, is to: (a) play _____ music
          NOUN   ADJECTIVE

   and see if they start _____ or (b) ask them to
                          VERB ENDING IN "ING"

   _____ a spell with their magical _____ .
        VERB   NOUN

2. If you meet someone who _____ like a vampire,
                              VERB ENDING IN "S"

   you should: (a) throw cold _____ on them and see if they
                                TYPE OF LIQUID

   _____ or (b) rub some _____ on their
        VERB   TYPE OF FOOD

   _____ , since real vampires _____ garlic.
   PART OF THE BODY   VERB

If you guessed *b* for both questions, congratulations—you can tell the

real thing from a/an _____ !
                          NOUN